THIS BOOK

belongs to

○ ○ ○ ○ ○ ○ ○ ○ ○ ○ ○ ○ ○ ○ ○ ○ ○ ○ ○

NUMBERS

1 2 3

4 5 6

7 8 9

10

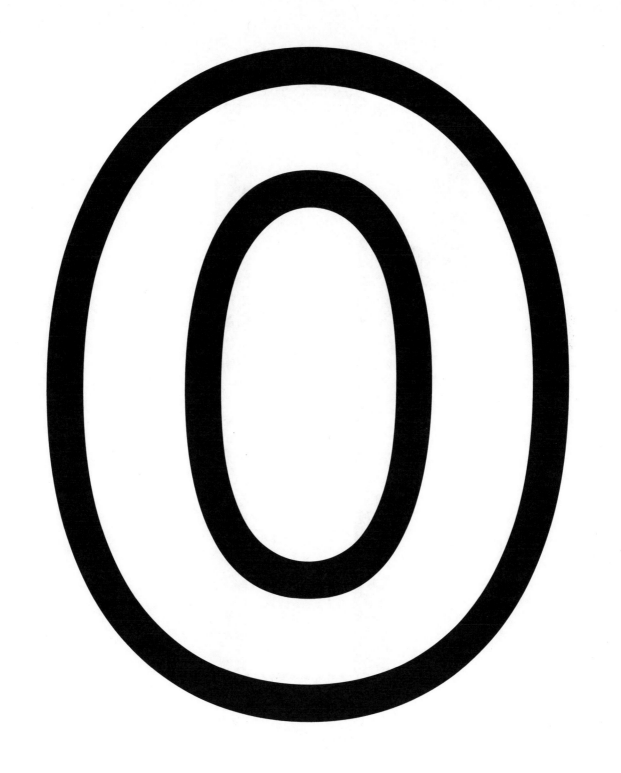

ZERO

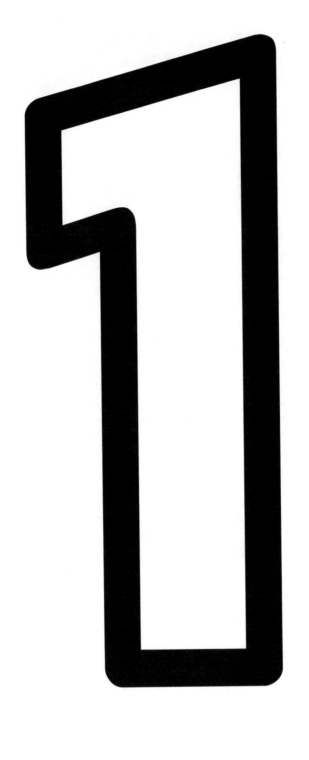

ONE

ONE

TWO

2

TWO

THREE

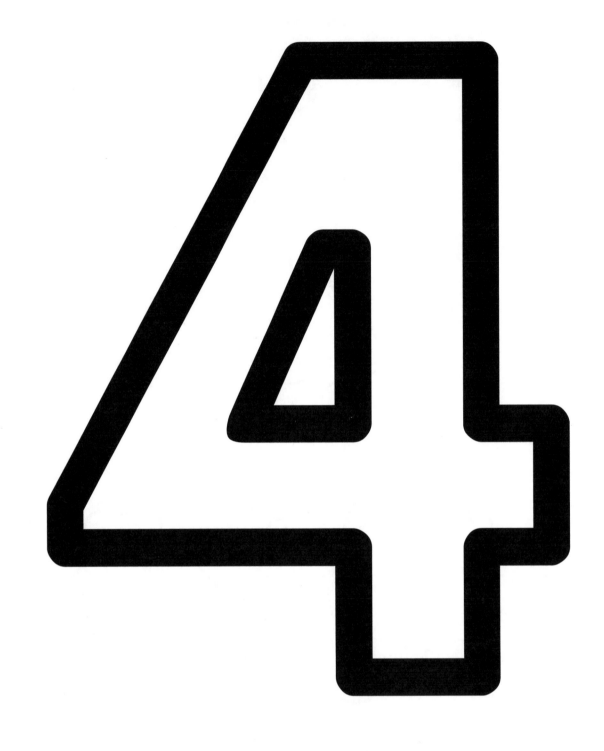

FOUR

4

FOUR

FIVE

5

FIVE

SIX

6

SIX

SEVEN

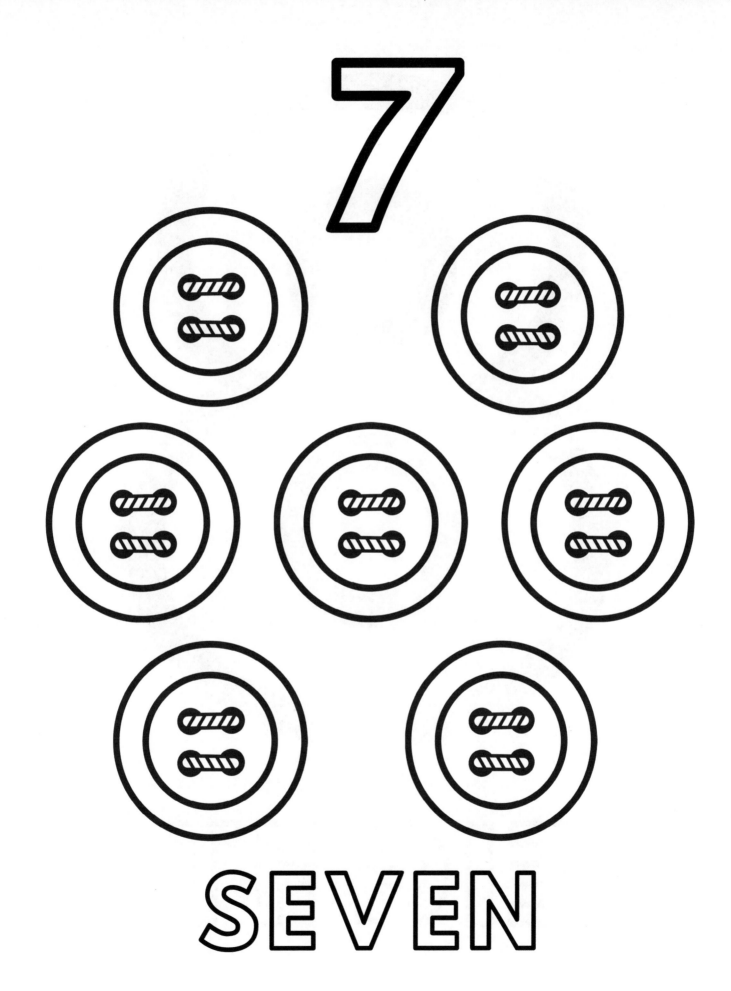

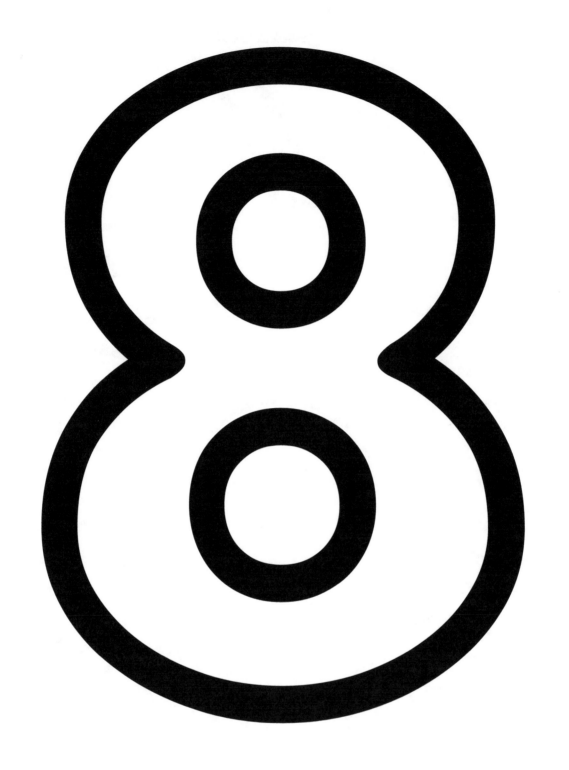

EIGHT

8

EIGHT

NINE

9

NINE

10

TEN

10

TEN

SHAPES

CIRCLE

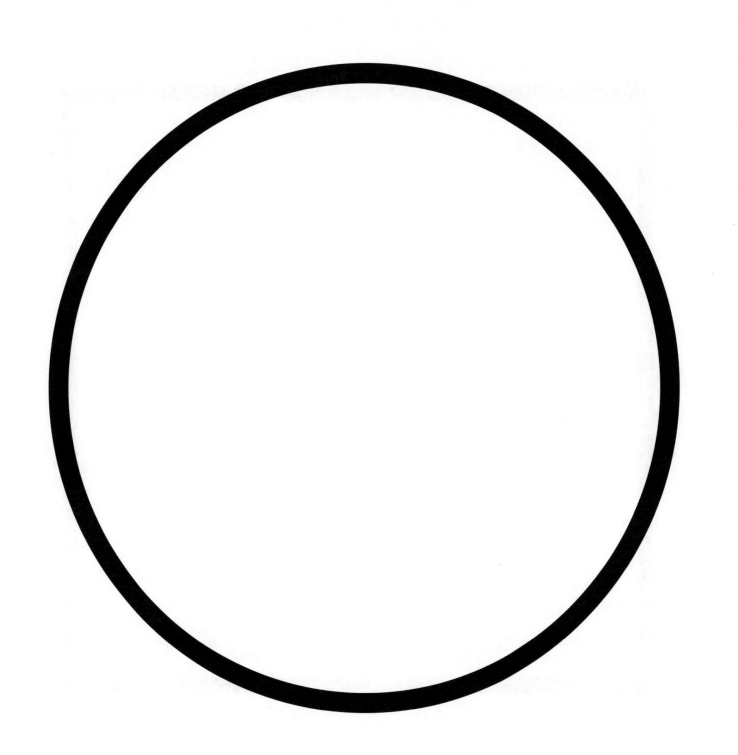

SQUARE

TRIANGLE

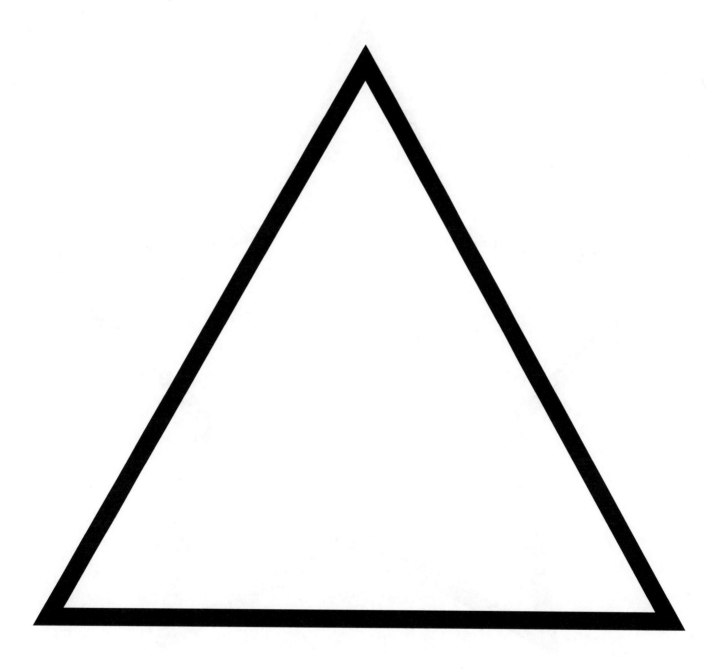

STAR

HEART

OVAL

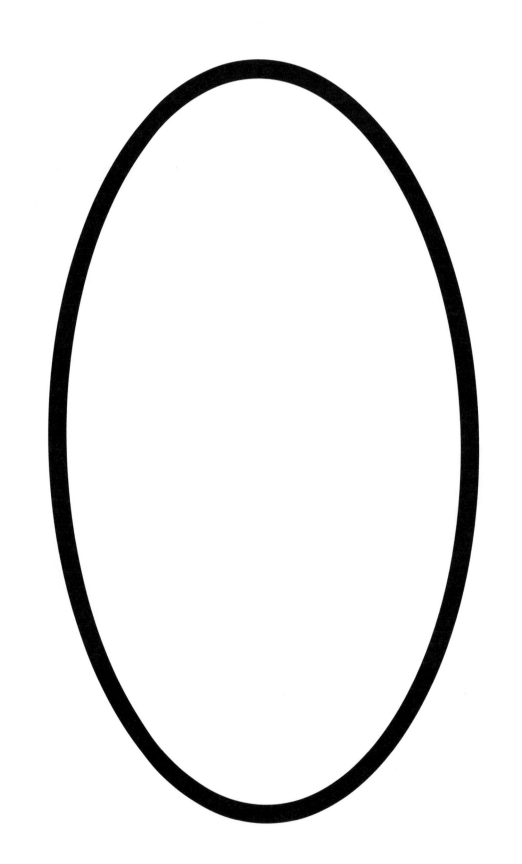

DIAMOND

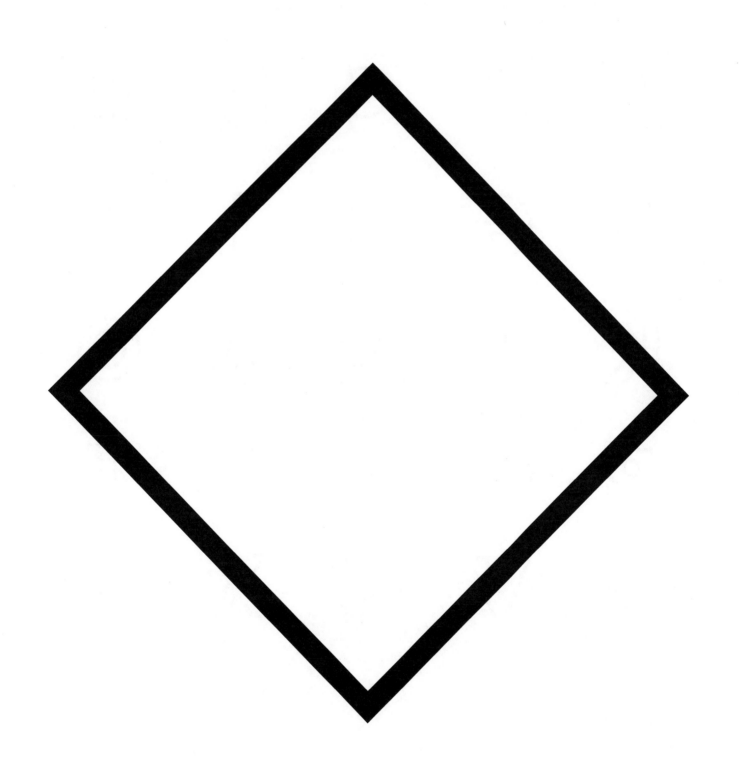

ALPHABET

A B C D E

F G H I J

K L M N O

P Q R S T

U V W X Y

Z

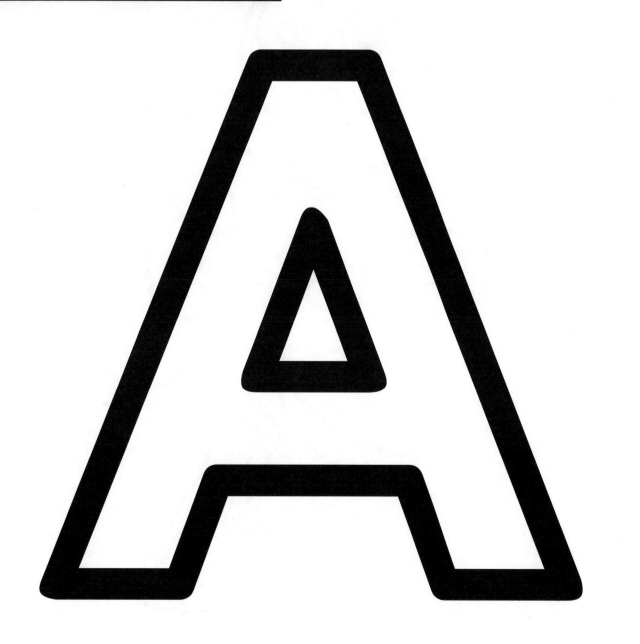

ANT

A

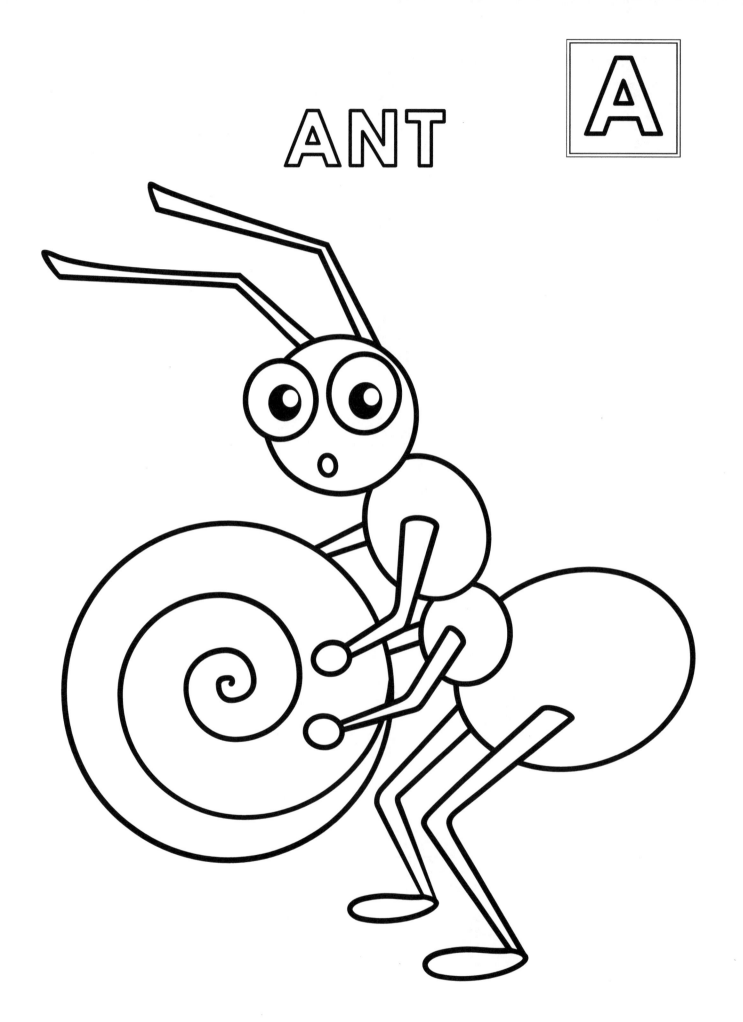

APPLE

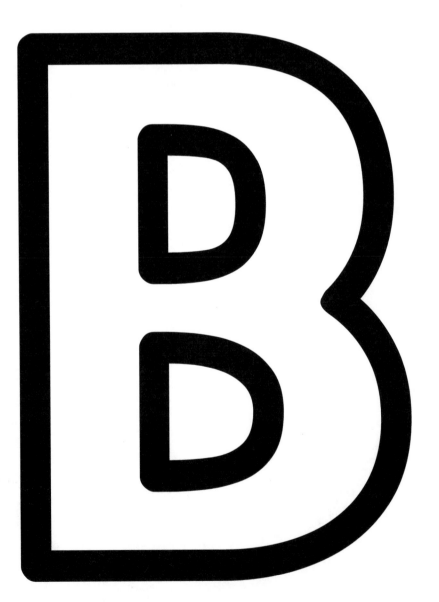

BUTTERFLY B

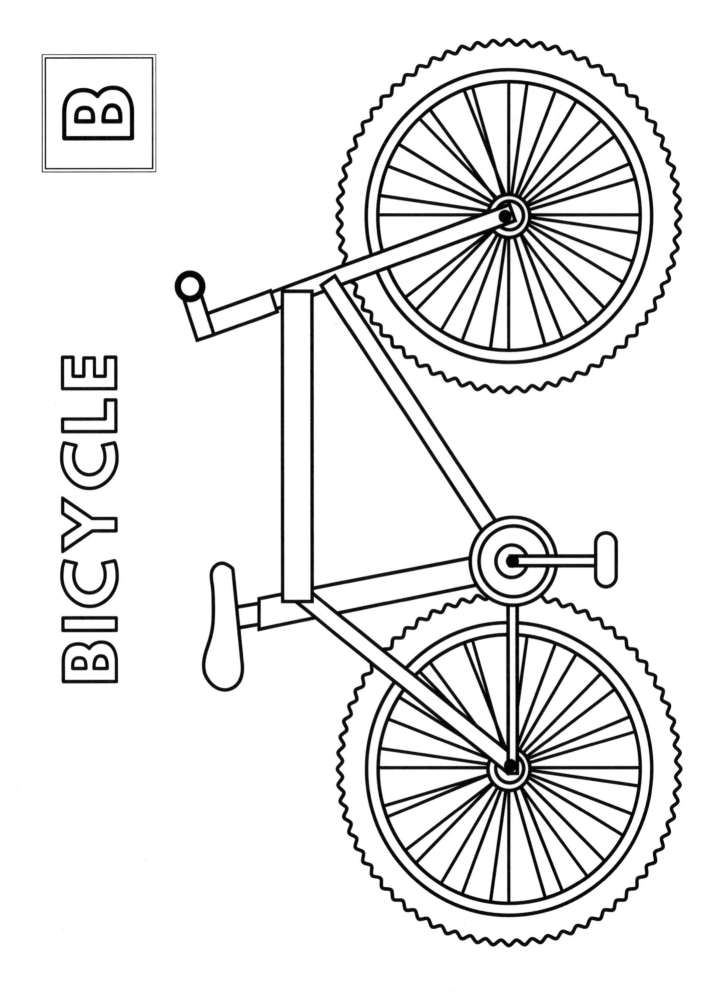

B

BICYCLE

BROCCOLI

B

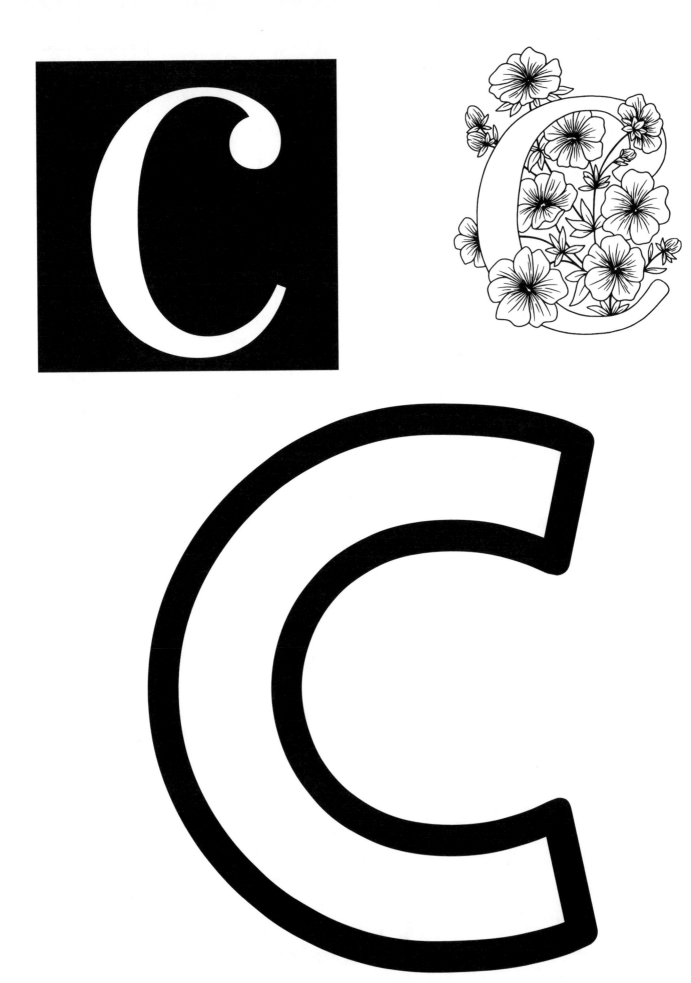

CLOCK

CAT

C

CAR

d

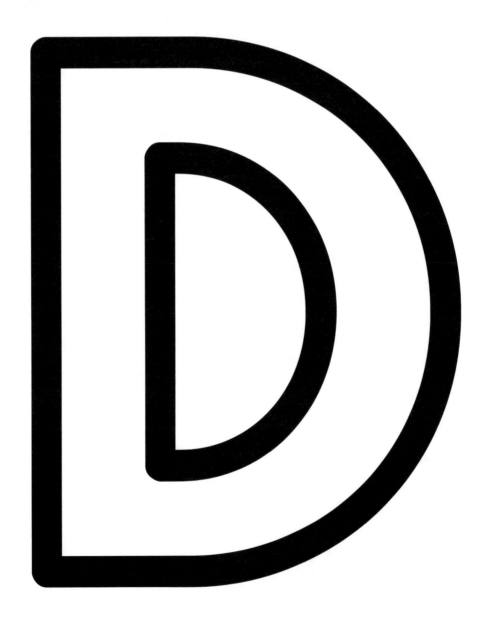

DOG

DIGGER

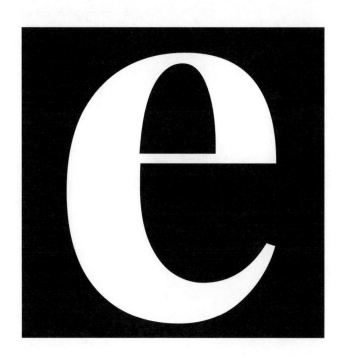

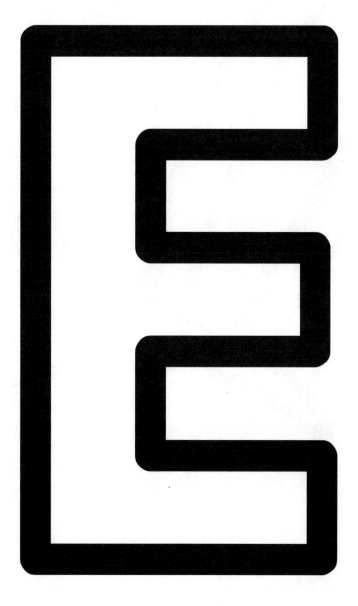

EARS

EGGS

E

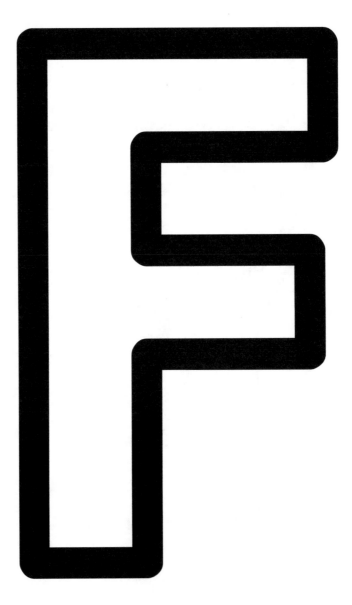

FLOWER

F

FISH

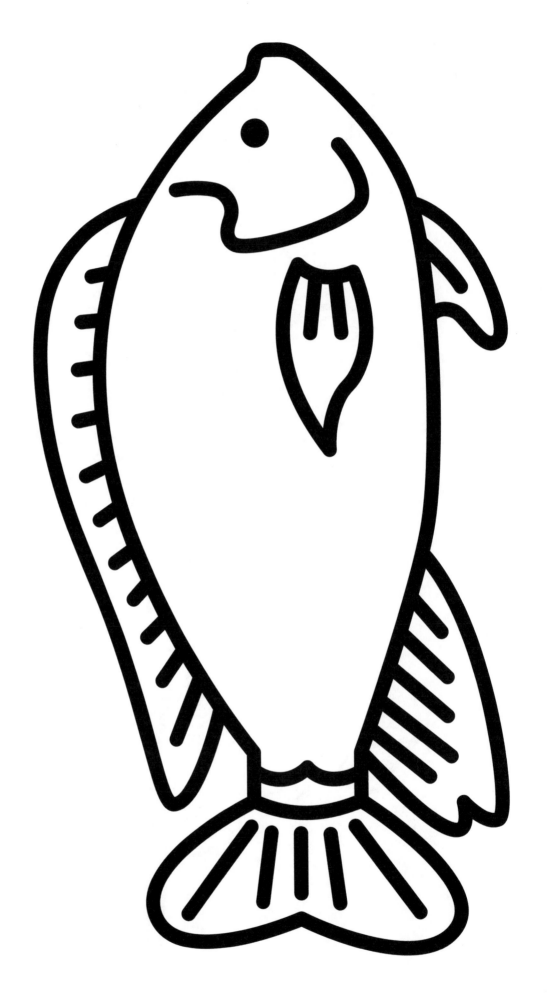

GLOVES

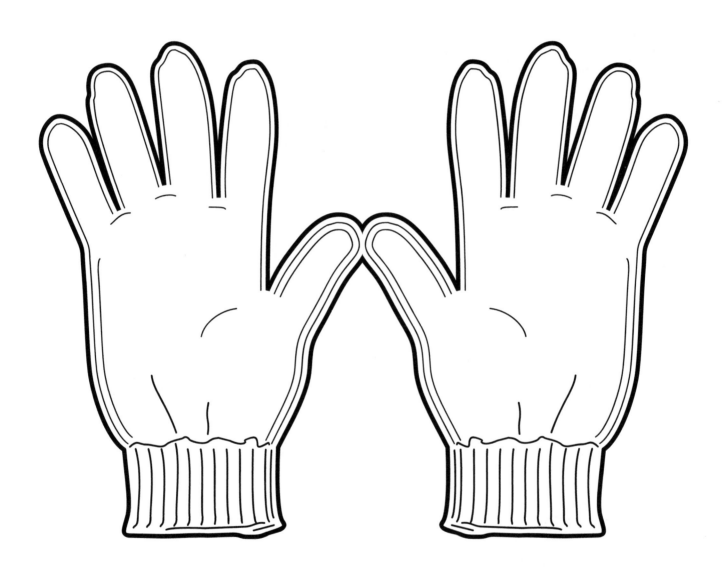

GUITAR

G

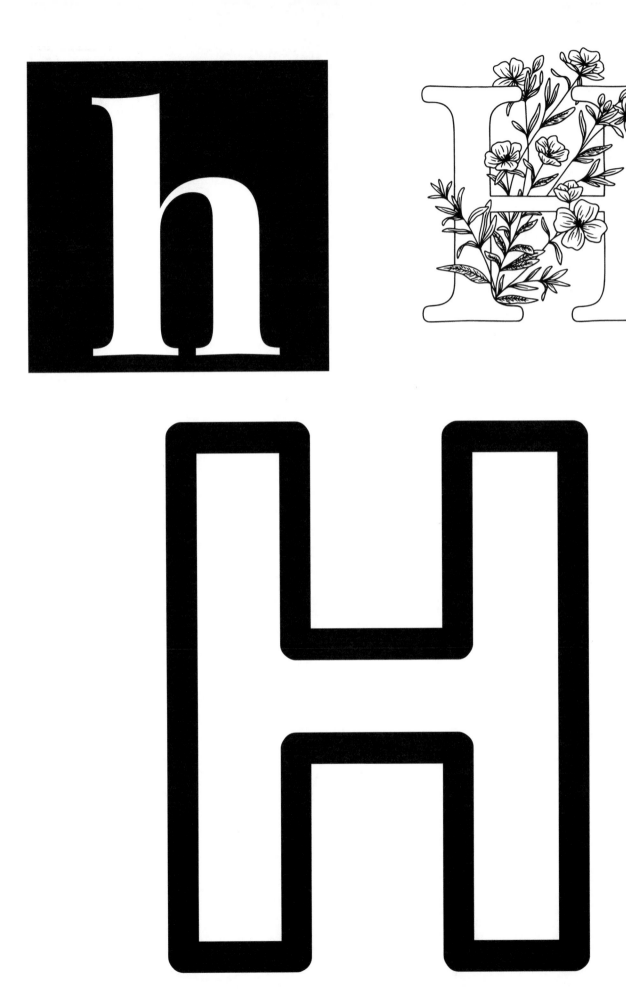

HORSE

HOUSE

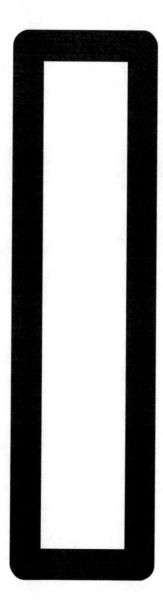

ICE CREAM

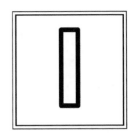

IRON

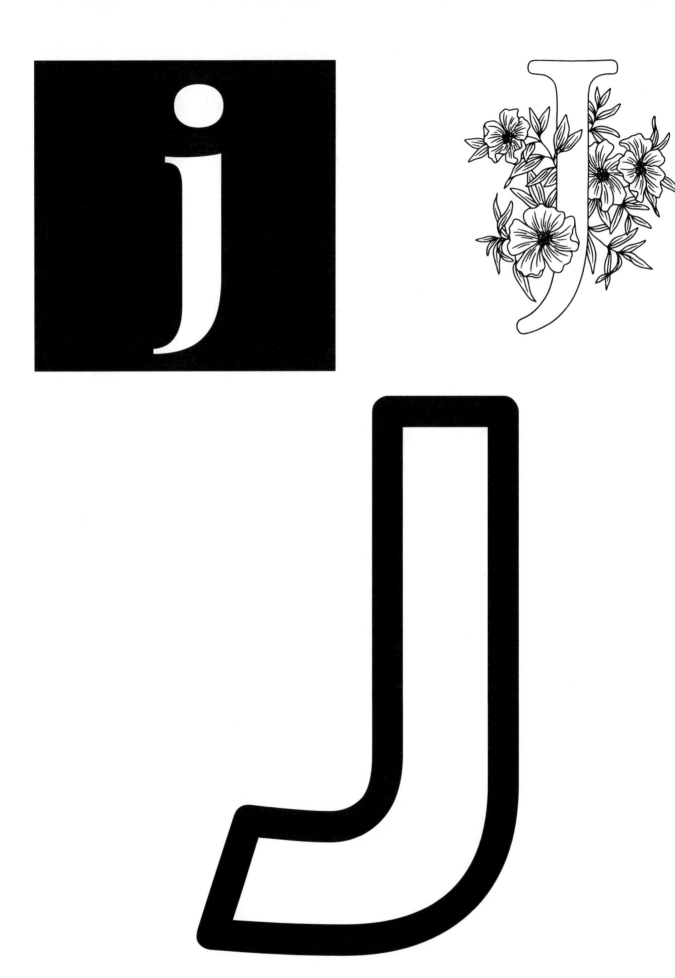

JET

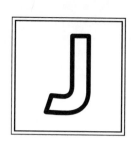

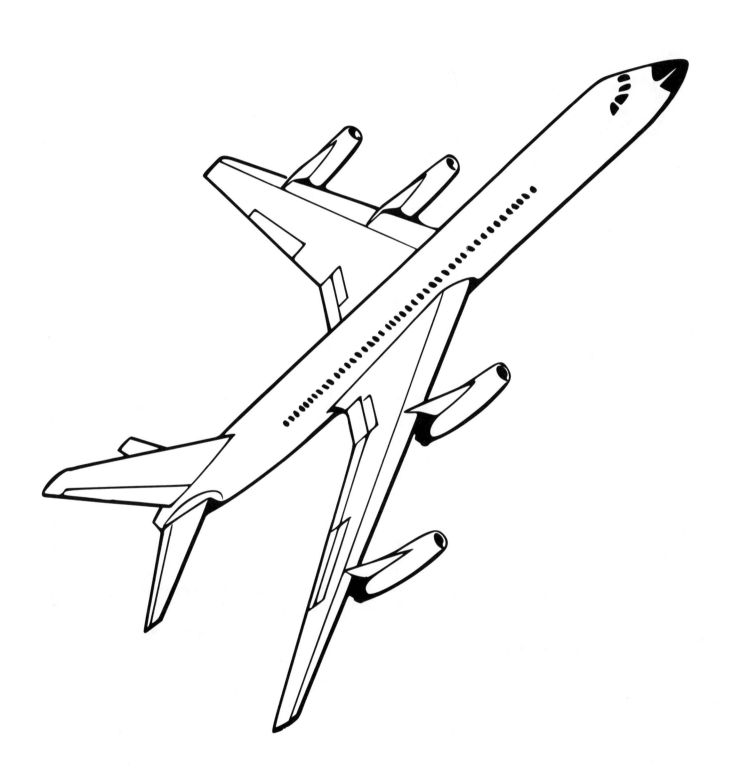

JAR

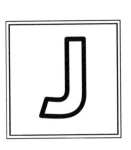

k

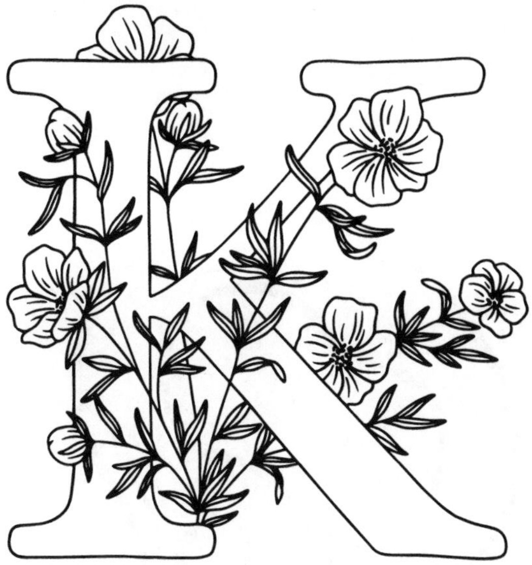

K

KEY

K

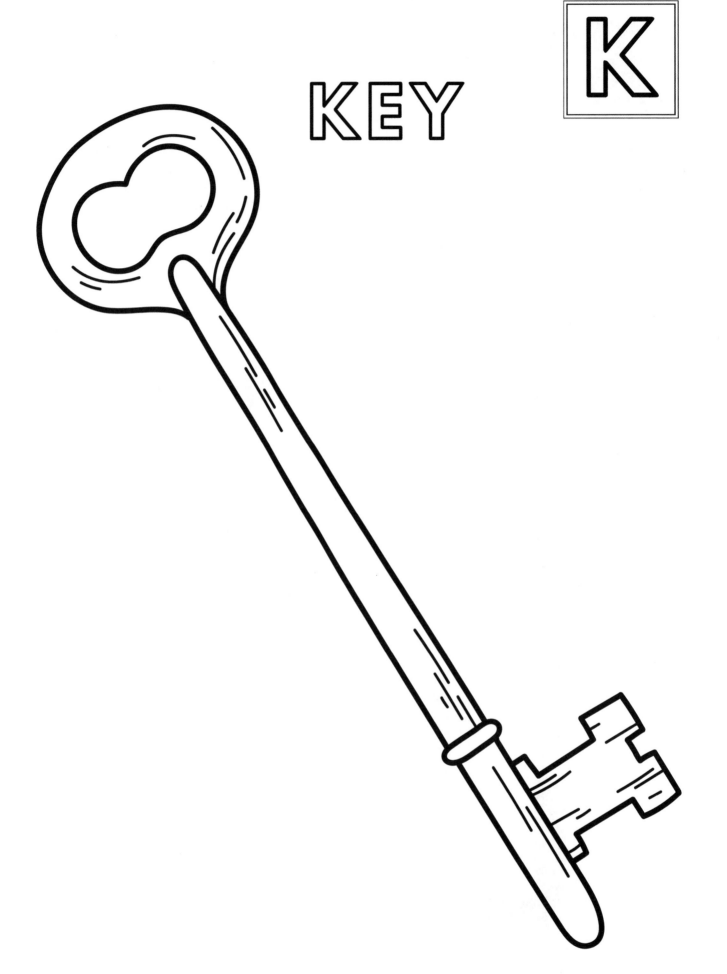

KETTLE

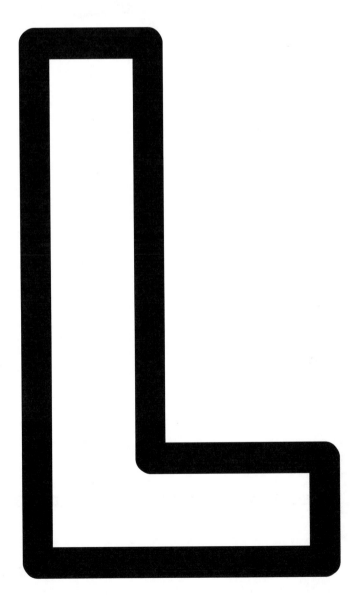

LETTUCE

L

LION

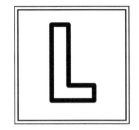

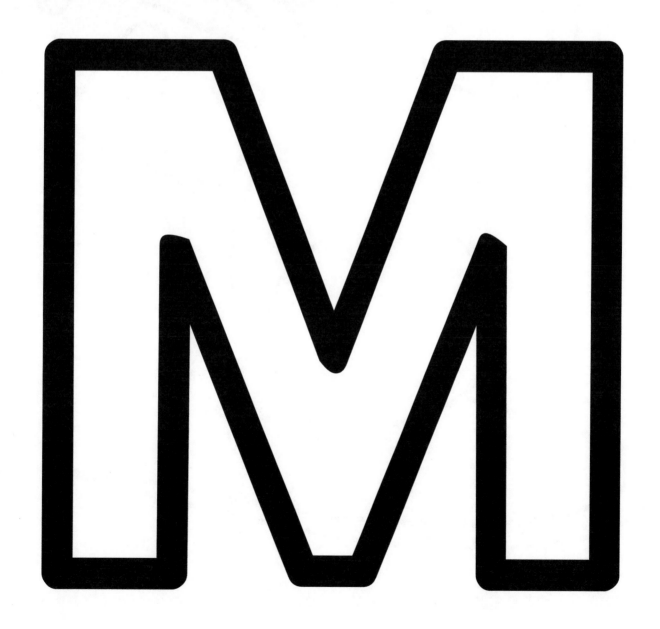

MOUSE

MOTHER

NURSE

NEST

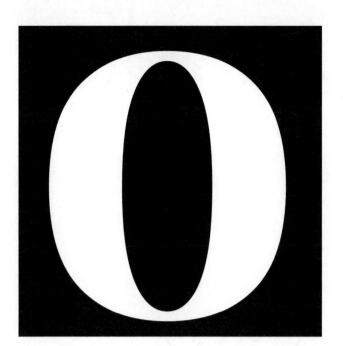

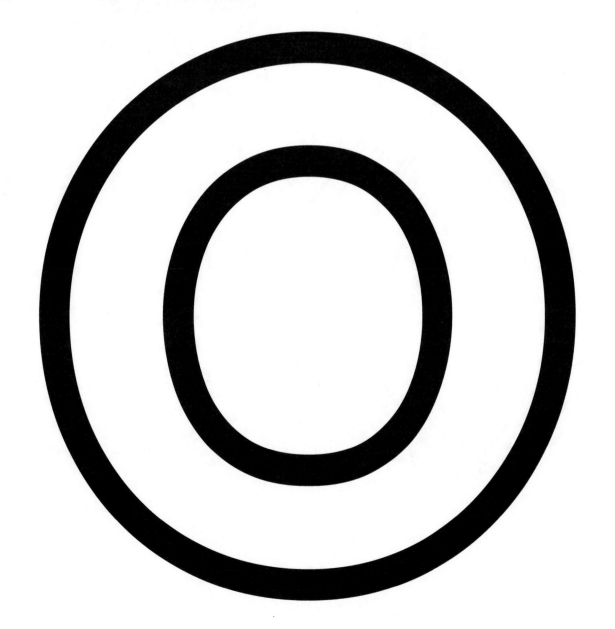

ONION

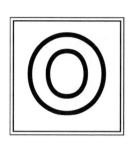

OWL
O

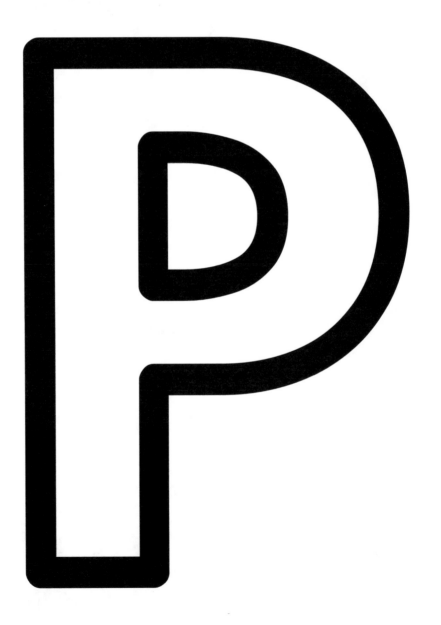

PANTS

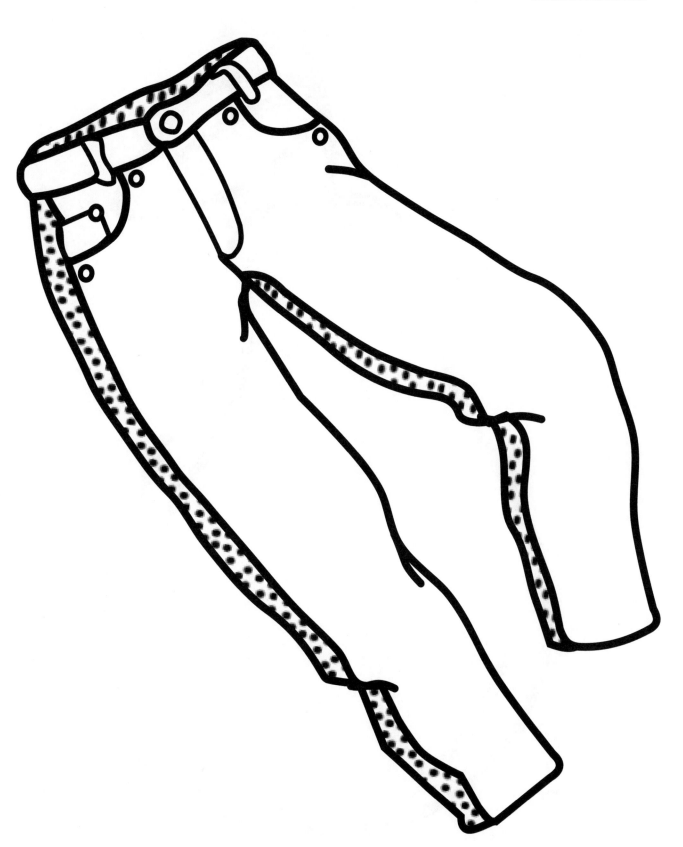

PEAR

QUEEN

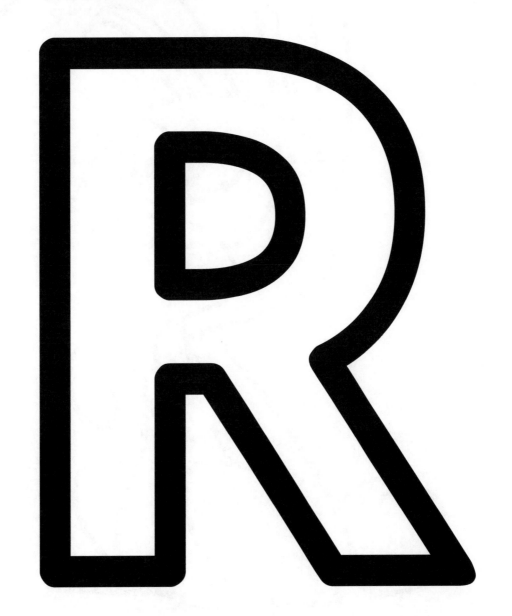

RABBIT

R

RUBBER BOOTS

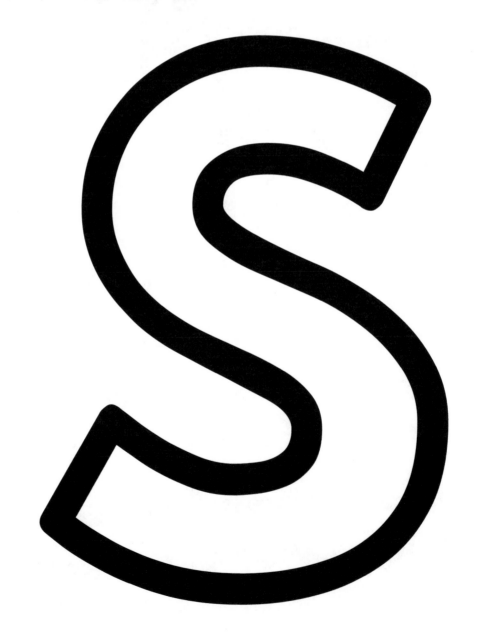

SLIDE

S

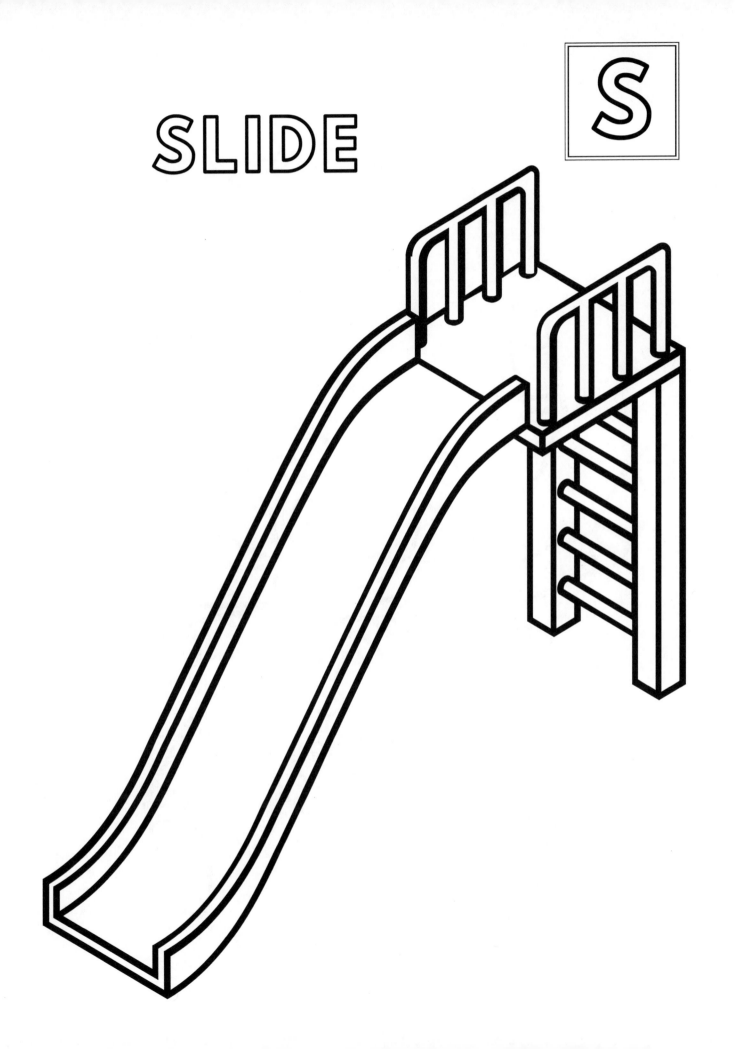

SPIDER

SHOES

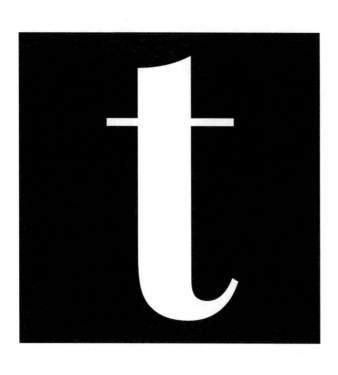 

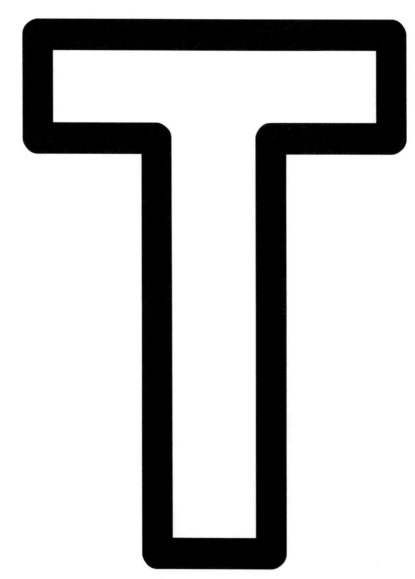

TEDDY BEAR

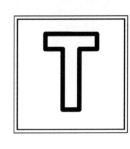

TREE

TONGUE

T

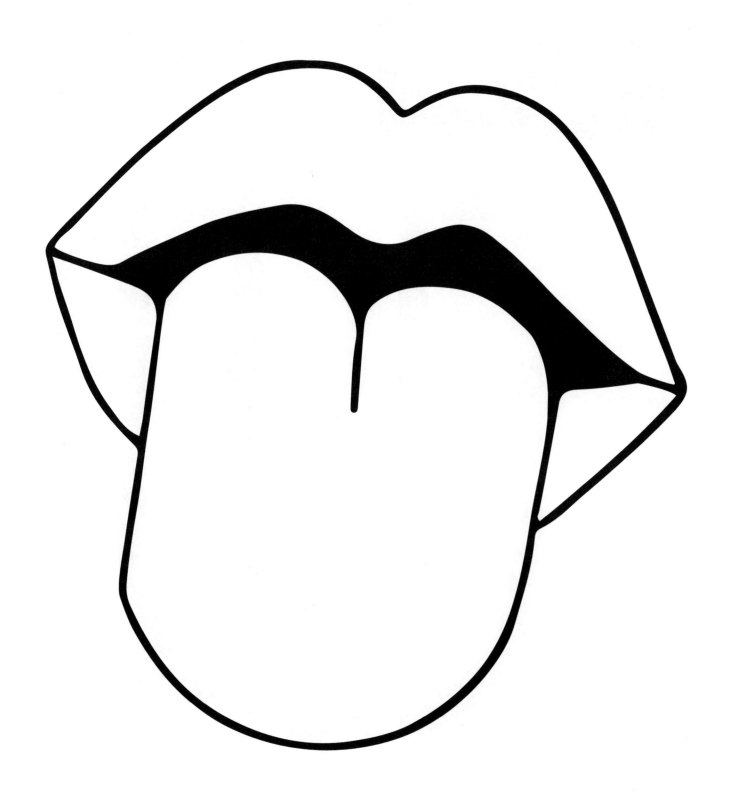

UMBRELLA

UNIFORM

VACUUM CLEANER

V

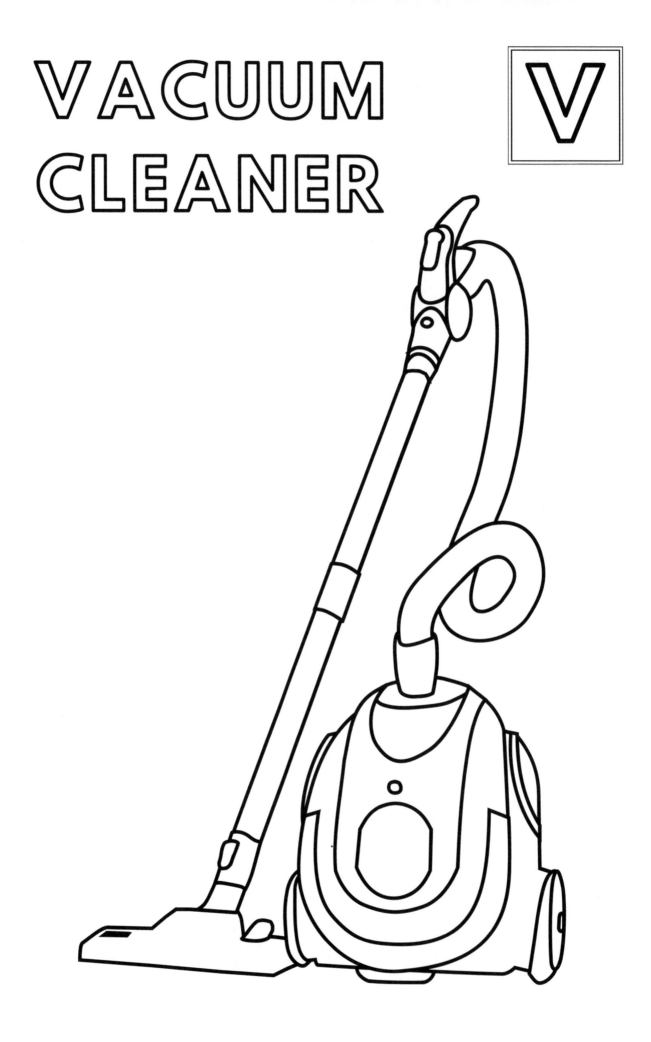

VAN

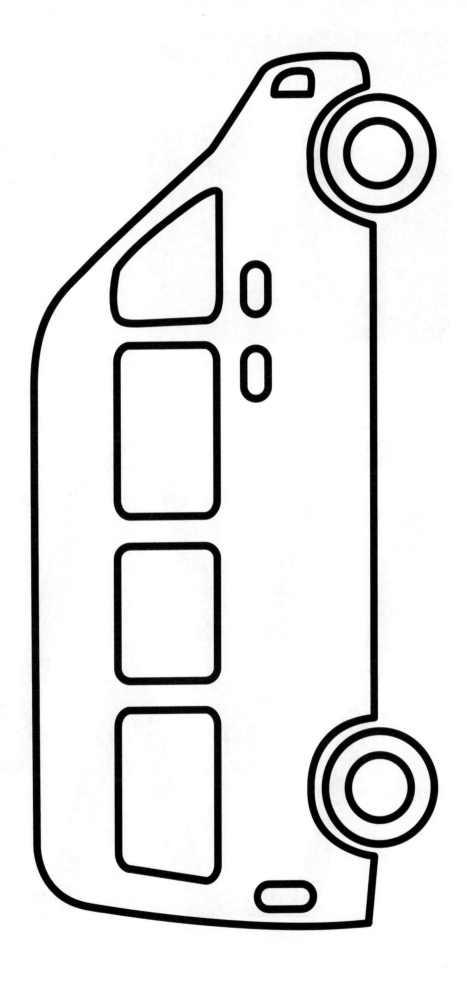

WASHING MACHINE

WARDROBE

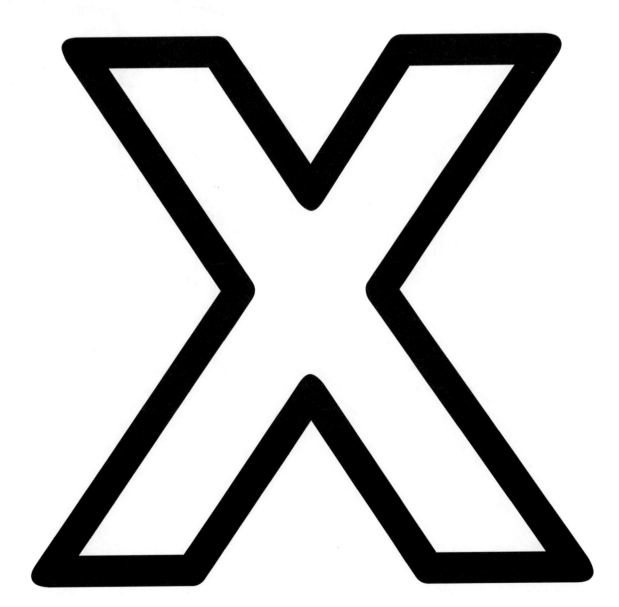

XYLOPHONE

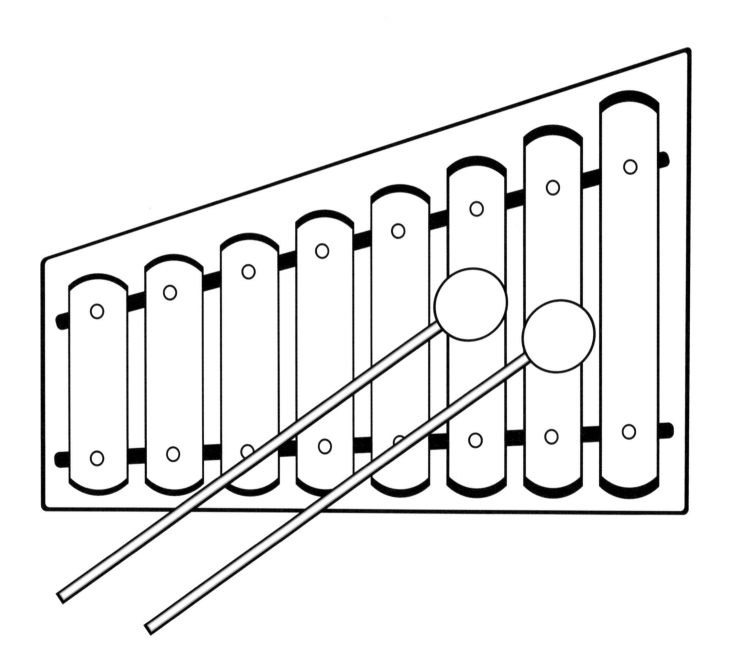

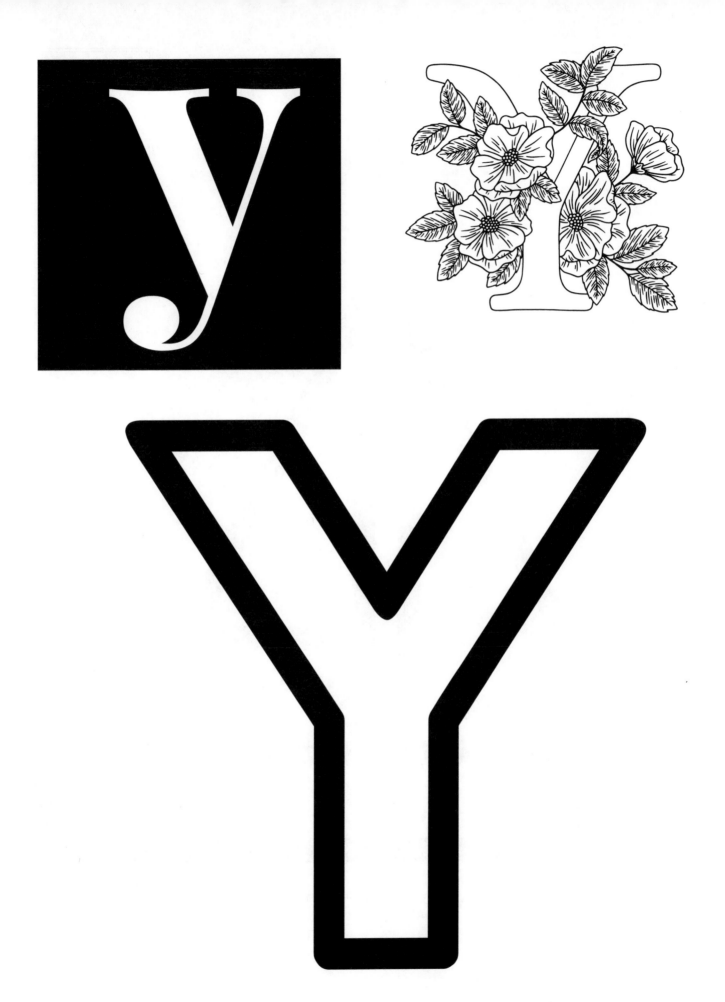

YACHT

Z

ZEBRA

Z

ZIP